# LAURA BOHN

## WAYS OF SEEING

# LAURA BOHN

## WAYS OF SEEING

LAURA BOHN WITH
PETER WEBSTER AND WENDY SILVERSTEIN

POINTED LEAF
PRESS

CONTENTS

INTERIOR DESIGN
$5.00
1985
A CAHNERS PUBLICATION
SECOND 100 INTERIOR DESIGN GIANTS
APARTMENT BY LEMBO-BOHN
HEXTER AWARDS 1985
ATTITUDES TOWARD THE PAST

# FOREWORD

I clearly remember, as if it were yesterday, October 2000, when Laura Bohn's stunning Manhattan duplex apartment was published in *House Beautiful.* I still recall turning the page to that first look—the amazing colors, the sense of scale and proportion, including her love of oversize pillows, 26 x 30! About those colors, they're really off-colors: grays that work with greens, browns with golden ochers. Laura is the true "Queen of Soft Modern," a title *Interior Design* coined for her years ago. She is an amazing high/low master, not afraid to get her hands dirty discovering hidden gems anywhere.

It's my immense pleasure not only to know Laura as a dear friend and as an *Interior Design* Hall of Fame member but also to publish her stellar work. I remember fondly the photo shoot for an enormous family beach house in the Rockaways, that playful attic bedroom with the row of twin beds on wheels, and how the two of us ran ourselves ragged until sunset. And who could forget photographing her own glorious country house in Pennsylvania? She and her husband, Richard, pretty much rebuilt the place brick by brick. (Her secret weapon: a husband who can build anything...and actually does.)

Back when Laura was a student, at Pratt, her own icons and mentors were Joseph D'Urso and John Saladino. To this day, she thinks BIG, and she lives it, too. She loves life! She still gets enthused, with a child's delight, and I think that is our connection. We are two kindred beings, head-over-heels for design. She is boundlessly passionate. Her favorite phrase tells you a thing or two about her spirit: "Isn't it fabulous?!" And we can't forget her generosity, from single-handedly putting together a whole wedding for one of her staff, in her barn, to surprising me with the exact gray-purple shade of nail polish that she knows we are both obsessed with, among many other generous gifties. Her thoughtfulness in caring for all the people around her makes her an amazing partner, friend, and designer for her clients.

As I pen this note, Laura's studio is chockablock with new projects, including a Connecticut house with a record 15 bathrooms. Then there's the chateau that she and Richard are looking to buy and renovate in Normandy, France. Wowza. Oh, and typical generous Laura, she wants to bring her friends. The unstoppable Laura and her insatiable appetite for *more.* More adventures, life experiences, and design challenges. You must agree she is one-of-a-kind striking, straight-shooting, chic, and, using her favorite word, *fabulous!*—Cindy Allen/Editor in chief, *Interior Design*

# BEGINNINGS

People often ask me how I became an interior designer. My path to the profession was circuitous—I didn't go to design school until I was in my thirties—but my love affair with design and architecture started early, when I was a young girl growing up in baby-boom Texas.

My mother, who had trained as a fashion illustrator at what is now ArtCenter College of Design in Pasadena, was that 1950s archetype, a fabulously talented woman who had given up the possibility of a career to marry and raise a family. That didn't mean her education and skills were wasted: She simply poured her creative know-how and energy into homemaking and became a sort of superhero version of the All-American Betty Crocker mom.

When it came to decorating our house, however, many of my mother's ideas were far from conventional. For instance, she installed dark gray industrial carpet and a bright pink sofa in our living room, a striking scheme for the time that not only raised the eyebrows of our many suburban Houston neighbors, most of whom favored shag rugs and pastel colors, but also instigated my lifelong passion for gray in all its shades and guises. (To this day, it remains my very favorite color—or, more properly, non-color—the one I probably use the most, an unfailing classic that's always in style.) My mother could be startlingly irreverent, too, blithely cutting down the legs of our 18th-century dining table—inherited from my grandmother!—and Chippendale-style chairs so they sat low to the ground, another effect that often drew comments from puzzled visitors.

Not that any of this disconcerted me. I loved living in a house that didn't look or feel like anyone else's. It also made me fascinated with the way other people lived and decorated. When visiting friends, I would carefully take note of everything in the house and then painstakingly describe all that I had seen to my mother when I got home. I was particularly struck by anything novel or unexpected, such as the real wax-candle sconces that lighted the paintings in an artsy household I went to for a birthday party. They made a deep impression, as magical to a little girl as the candelabra-holding human arms projecting from the castle walls in Jean Cocteau's 1946 film *Beauty and the Beast*.

My father, an engineer, played an equally crucial role in my early design education. Among the projects he headed were the mammoth heating, cooling, and electrical

systems for the Astrodome, the crown jewel of mid-century Houston's space-age aspirations. He also acted as the architect on a new house my family built when I was about 10 years old. I was intrigued by the plans, which were often spread across the kitchen table. My father not only taught me how to read them, he also allowed me to make changes to the layouts. One of these involved moving the living room fireplace into a corner—a bad idea, as it turned out, but there it sits to this day—to make space for a banquette in my adjacent bedroom. My mother used a vividly patterned purple fabric I had chosen to upholster the banquette, the overhead valence, and my little bed, so they all matched.

But as much as I was delighted by the decorative results of the project, the design process captivated me even more—seeing how ideas worked out on paper could determine the look and feel of the space I lived in. From then on, I began drawing house plans compulsively, an amusement I continued through high school and on to college at the University of Texas at Austin. I would send the drawings home to my mother, who would critique them and send them back. Always a terrible student—school had never engaged me, and college was no different—I flunked out after a year. My parents, of course, were horrified, but neither they nor I recognized what seems obvious now: My talents and interests were pointing me toward a career in interior design. But even if we had realized what I should be studying, the University of Texas, Austin—now considered one of the best schools for aspiring designers—offered no design major back then.

The profession didn't really exist as such in Eisenhower-era America. We were still in the age of "interior decorators," most of them women with no formal training to speak of, who parlayed their personal taste and social connections into businesses. Some were influential—talents like Elsie de Wolfe and Dorothy Draper, who did for decorating between the wars what Coco Chanel did for fashion—but in the absence of schools or certification programs, "lady decorators" were often looked on as gifted dilettantes who didn't do much beyond choose fabrics and arrange furniture for their well-heeled friends.

That condescending view would gradually change over the next decade or so. The introduction of formal educational requirements and the proliferation of reputable courses and institutions turned the vaguely amateur "interior decorator" into the thoroughly professional "interior designer," while the increasing number of men entering the field helped remove the sexist pejorative that it was only "women's work." Billy Baldwin, perhaps the greatest influence on the first generation of post-

PAGE 6: LEMBO-BOHN DESIGN ASSOCIATES CREATED A LOCATION SET FOR THE 1985 MOVIE *THE YEAR OF THE DRAGON* THAT BECAME THE COVER OF *INTERIOR DESIGN* IN DECEMBER 1985. PAGE 8: AS A FIVE YEAR OLD IN HOUSTON, TEXAS, I AM WEARING A WHITE PLEATED SKIRT AND PINK SWEATER SELECTED BY MY STYLISH GRANDMOTHER WHO OFTEN WORE DIAMONDS AND GRAY FLANNEL SUITS. LEFT: I WORE A NINA RICCI PLEATED PINK DRESS FOR A FASHION SHOW HELD AT THE CASINO DE MONTE-CARLO IN MONACO, BEFORE A PERFORMANCE BY THE FRENCH SINGER CHARLES AZNAVOUR. OPPOSITE AND ABOVE: THE HEADSHOTS WERE ALSO TAKEN THAT EVENING.

LEFT: I LOVE DISPLAYING FAMILY PHOTOGRAPHS. ONE OF MY FAVORITES IS OF ME AS A YOUNG CHILD WITH MY RAGGEDY ANN AND ANDY DOLLS THAT MY GRANDMOTHER HAD MADE. BELOW: THE PORTRAIT OF ME IN A BRIGHT BLUE DRESS IN BOARDING SCHOOL WAS TAKEN WHEN I WAS 15 YEARS OLD.

ABOVE: HERE I AM PICTURED WITH RICHARD FIORE, MY BOYFRIEND AT THE TIME. WE POSED FOR THE PHOTOGRAPHER MARCUS LEATHERDALE IN OUR FIRST MANHATTAN LOFT, COMPLETE WITH FASHIONABLE WALL-TO-WALL CARPETING ON EVERY SURFACE. I WORE A BRONZE LEATHER TOP AND RICHARD WORE A BLACK SHIRT WITH A METALLIC VEST, STANDARD PERIOD ATTIRE. OPPOSITE: AFTER SPENDING THE DAY DRIVING HIS TRACTOR ON OUR PROPERTY IN OTTSVILLE, BUCKS COUNTY, PENNSYLVANIA, RICHARD APPEARED WITH A BUNCH OF LILACS TO APPEASE ME.

World War II American interior designers, countered such prejudices in his own way: Although he had studied architecture at Princeton University, in Princeton, New Jersey, for two years, he actively disdained the term "designer" and always unapologetically referred to himself as a "decorator."

All this was *terra incognita* to me, and it would be several years before I recognized interior design as a career possibility. What I did instead was to become a model, not such an out-of-left-field idea since many people had suggested it to me as a rail-thin, fashion-crazy teenager. (I had even taken classes at a local modeling school, where that delicious cliché, a big black-patent-leather hatbox, was deemed an obligatory accessory.) A friend living in New York City needed a roommate, so I went there, found an agent, and immediately began getting jobs as a house model for different manufacturers on Seventh Avenue. The work was not glamorous, but it paid the rent, and within three or four years, I had my own apartment on the parlor floor of a 19th-century brownstone near Gramercy Park.

Of course, I decorated my new home—a beautiful, high-ceilinged, two-room space with great light and a fireplace—avoiding trendy Pop Art flourishes or flower-child psychedelics in favor of a pared-down environment in the gray, white, and taupe palette that I still use today. My boldest moves were to use brown patent leather to upholster the kitchen banquette and deep-chestnut linen to re-upholster a pair of Regency-style chairs I'd bought on sale from the Plaza Hotel. The makeover got so many compliments that another model and I decided to moonlight as a decorating team, though in truth neither of us knew how to do anything. We printed up cards, told all our friends, and were soon hired to do over yet another model's apartment. She was a German with dramatic looks and avant-garde tastes, so we gave her a massive tufted leather sofa, painted the walls paper-bag brown, and hung up huge Expressionist posters. The results were good enough to have set us up on a more serious footing, but a chance invitation to cross the Atlantic on the *MS Gripsholm*, a wonderfully sleek Swedish-American ocean liner, offered me more immediate gratification. So, with no plan in mind, I sailed to Sweden and from there, took the train to meet friends in Paris.

Like every young American, I was stunned and enchanted by the City of Light, deciding on the spot that I had to get a job and live there. To my delight, modeling allowed me to do just that for three glorious years. Clutching a letter of introduction from New York, I applied to be an *haute-couture* house model at Christian Dior, where I was interviewed by Marc Bohan himself. I thought the couturier just about

WORLD THEATER

PREVIOUS PAGES: THE LOCATION SET FOR THE 1985 MOVIE *THE YEAR OF THE DRAGON* WAS CREATED BY LEMBO-BOHN DESIGN ASSOCIATES, TURNING RAW SPACE IN A BROOKLYN INDUSTRIAL BUILDING INTO A GLAMOROUS LOFT WITH REAL VIEWS OF THE MANHATTAN BRIDGE AND MIDTOWN SKYLINE. ABOVE: OUR LEMBO-BOHN DESIGN ASSOCIATES OFFICE AT 1 GANSEVOORT STREET WAS AMONG THE FIRST BUSINESSES TO MOVE INTO MANHATTAN'S STILL-INDUSTRIAL MEAT-PACKING DISTRICT. WE OCCUPIED THE SPACE FOR 16 YEARS.

the most soigné man I'd ever met. What made an even bigger and, for the future designer, more important impression on me, however, was the Avenue Montaigne townhouse's impossibly chic and enduringly famous pale gray-and-white décor. Often dubbed "Dior Gray," the pearly shade is actually *gris Trianon*, named for Marie Antoinette's exquisite little 18th-century chateau at Versailles, where it was used extensively. Dior adopted it as an exemplar of the Louis XVI style, which he adored, and used it on the salon's walls to help create the "decorated but not decorative" atmosphere he wanted. Drinking in the sense of calm and order conjured by the ethereal color—it really allowed the proportions and details of the neoclassical architecture to shine through—I thought back to my mother's charcoal living-room carpet, and had a small epiphany about gray's chameleon nature and the diverse design possibilities that it offered.

I didn't get the job at Dior, but ended up as an *haute-couture* model at Nina Ricci, instead. It was a world away from Seventh Avenue—no ready-to-wear, just exquisite designs, made-to-order for private clients, cut and sewn in-house, and featuring the most extraordinary fabrics and meticulous detailing. Each model had a collection made on her—10 to 12 styles, from tailored suits to gorgeous evening wear, that fit her look and personality—which she would show customers in the salon. In the evenings, we were required to attend swank social events such as the opera, where, swathed in silk and chinchilla, we sat on display in the velvet-swagged boxes. It was like being in a Balzac novel. Having been at the salon since dawn, most of us were dog tired. I'd often slip out mid-performance, put my glamorous attire in a box, get on a bus, and ride home exhausted to bed.

Home was a beautiful high-ceilinged room with its own balcony that I rented in a family apartment in the 3rd arrondissement. I grew to love the quirks and pleasures of the French bourgeois lifestyle, not least its delicious food. I put on weight and, considered too fat for the Paris salon, was banished to the provincial fashion circuit. This involved a small caravan of cars, stuffed with clothes and models, traveling from town to town to put on shows. It was a grueling but also exhilarating experience in that the more I saw of France, the more I adored its people, culture, and countryside. The hard work also meant that after a few months on the road I lost those offending pounds and was allowed back to Paris.

The modeling life does not last forever, and I had been on the job full-time for 11 years. So, as we entered the 1970s, I decided to return to New York and take stock of my options. Everything changed very rapidly. I married my first husband, James Bohn, an extraordinarily talented Madison Avenue art director with a wide range of intellectual and cultural interests, who would be a strong influence on me. As was the women's consciousness-raising group I joined at the time. The second-wave feminist movement was at its fabulous, bra-burning zenith, and all eight or nine members of my group were professional working women—attorneys, graphic designers, teachers—who thought modeling was ridiculous and insisted that I go back to school and learn how to do something worthwhile. So, at the age of 32, despite my disastrous academic record, I enrolled at Pratt Institute, a haven for students interested in the fine and applied arts.

Using my freshman year to explore the possibilities Pratt offered, I attended a presentation on what was then called the Environmental Design program. It was a true *aha* moment. As explained, the department's approach to interior design was very architectural in a way that made perfect sense to me, and I came out of that talk knowing without a doubt I had found my major. It was exactly the sort of academic course that, had it been offered at UT Austin, might have jump-started my design career a decade earlier.

I had the enormous good fortune to get the legendary designer Joseph D'Urso as my first teacher at Pratt. D'Urso was a guru of high tech, the revolutionary 1970s design movement that stripped interiors down to their minimalist bones and outfitted them with industrial materials and furnishings sourced from restaurant supply stores, laboratory equipment outlets, institutional lighting catalogs, and other purveyors of commercial-grade finishes, fixtures, and fittings. His pared-down, achromatic spaces, with their glossy white walls, black leather and chrome furniture, gunmetal industrial appointments, and charcoal carpeting—yes, just like my mother's!—were a revelation and an inspiration. Here was a master giving permission to a novice to banish unnecessary clutter and splash her favorite non-color around.

But more important, under D'Urso's demanding tutelage, I learned how to think about color, texture, materiality, and every other applied element architecturally, as an integral part of the design rather than as mere decorative embellishment. We were taught to approach every project as a fundamental question of space—how to create it, control it, organize it, expand it, shrink it, energize it, tame it, make it bend to our will. I noticed almost immediately that my beloved gray was a very potent player in the game of manipulating space and that, unlike some other colors, it did so without ever becoming loud or aggressive.

It took me longer to master some of the other space-molding tools at the designer's disposal. D'Urso was maniacally insistent that every design decision be motivated by rigorous analysis. If you couldn't justify your proposal, he would say, "This is all arbitrary. There's got to be a watertight reason behind each choice you make." And then he'd rip up your plan or tear apart your model in front of the class. Quick, deep, and indelible, they were devastating but effective lessons. Once I got used to his drill sergeant teaching methods, D'Urso became my favorite professor and another seminal influence in my life.

Getting hired after I graduated proved relatively easy. Because I was older than most applicants, firms assumed I had much more experience and know-how than I did. That was the only reason I got my third job out of school—one for which I was underqualified—as a senior designer in the New York office of John Saladino, one of the most talented designers this country has produced. Saladino's work is opulent, colorful, and romantic, yet ordered, subtle, and restrained; Baudelaire's famous descriptive poetic refrain, *"luxe, calme et volupté,"* from *Fleurs du Mal* could have been written about his quietly sumptuous interiors.

My two years working for Saladino were as important to my education as my time at Pratt. They gave me a different but complementary perspective on the art of design. D'Urso was a purist who taught us to look at design almost in moral terms: Spare,

ABOVE AND LEFT: LAURA BOHN DESIGN ASSOCIATES WAS HEADQUARTERED ON SEVENTH AVENUE FOR MANY YEARS. I ENCLOSED MY PRIVATE OFFICE WITH SLATTED WOOD WALLS SO I COULD SEE EVERYONE WHILE WORKING. OVERLEAF: BEFORE MOVING INTO THE BANK BUILDING, WE LIVED IN A LOFT ON 26TH STREET IN MANHATTAN. WE SOLD THE PROPERTY COMPLETELY FURNISHED AND THEN JUST WALKED AWAY.

clean, and functional were his watchwords, and his interiors were as stripped-down and tough-minded as a Mondrian canvas. Saladino is as intellectually rigorous as D'Urso—there isn't an ounce of excess in his carefully controlled work, and his layouts are paragons of planning—but having trained as a painter at Yale, he is a sensualist, too. He approaches design like an artist, using color, light, shape, and texture to create luscious three-dimensional compositions. But underlying the surfaces in any Saladino room is a deep understanding of classical architecture, which gives the space a feeling of structure and discipline. And thanks to his familiarity with styles of every period, even his most contemporary schemes are infused with a palpable sense of history. These were qualities and values I recognized from the world of *haute couture*, and I soaked them in like a sponge.

Although it wasn't always clear to me at the time, I now realize that my subsequent career has been a process of integrating D'Urso's and Saladino's distinctive visions into a fully formed design sensibility of my own—a unique and personal way of seeing. Joseph Lembo, a gifted young designer who worked with me in Saladino's office, became a crucial part of that evolution. Joseph and I formed an instant rapport that soon grew into a near-telepathic connection—each could tell what the other thought about a design problem (or solution) before either had said a word. Our skill sets were complementary: Joseph had a passion for aesthetics and a marvelous sense of color and proportion, while I was always aware of the structural and architectural ramifications of a design, and found addressing mechanical and logistical issues endlessly fascinating. We both thought working for Saladino was a privilege, but we were both ready to move on. So, in 1980 we jumped ship together and, working on a shoestring budget, launched our own firm: Lembo-Bohn Design Associates. It was a fortunate move.

Maybe it was because we were the newest kids on the block, but almost immediately, Joseph and I began to get the most wonderful residential and commercial assignments in the United States, Europe, the Middle East, and Asia. Working with project architects, we designed five buildings from the ground up in Japan, including a gray pre-cast concrete restaurant complex in Nagoya that featured neoclassical cornices, moldings, and celadon-marble columns (it was the postmodernist era, after all); and a 3,000-square-foot pizza-and-pasta restaurant in Fukuoka that Joseph described to the *New York Times* as "a high-tech monastery." Retail and residential projects in Saudi Arabia followed, along with apartments, houses, stores, and offices stateside. We worked on the West Coast, too, doing an enormous house in Santa

PREVIOUS PAGE RIGHT: I DESIGNED THIS GLAMOROUS BATHROOM, COMPLETE WITH A BATHTUB AIRLIFTED FROM ITALY, IN COLLABORATION WITH ARCHITECT SCOTT BROMLEY OF BROMLEY CALDARI ARCHITECTS. THE PURCHASE, NEW YORK, PROJECT APPEARED IN *HOUSE BEAUTIFUL*. ABOVE AND LEFT: THE 19TH CENTURY BARN ON OUR PROPERTY IN OTTSVILLE, BUCKS COUNTY, SET THE STAGE FOR AN OVER-THE-TOP SURPRISE BIRTHDAY PARTY IN MY HONOR. OVERLEAF RIGHT: THIS IMAGE COMES FROM A STORY IN *INTERIOR DESIGN*. I WAS ONE OF SEVERAL DESIGNERS WHO WAS PROFILED WITH A FAVORITE PIECE OF FURNITURE.

Barbara for Susan Harris, the writer and producer of *The Golden Girls*, *Soap*, *Benson*, and other television hit comedies.

Lembo-Bohn even expanded into movie design when director Michael Cimino asked us to create a set for his 1985 neo-noir thriller *The Year of the Dragon*. Most of the picture was shot on sound stages in Wilmington, North Carolina, but for a central character's New York apartment, Cimino wanted vast windows with real views of the Manhattan skyline. So, for about a week's shooting, we converted 3,200 square feet of raw space on the top floor of a factory building in Brooklyn's Dumbo neighborhood into a glamorous open-plan loft. We treated it exactly as if it was one of our regular projects, with carpeted platforms, low, soft seating, a centrally placed bed on a raised sleeping area, and a spa-size tiled bathing pool. It looked as sensational in person as it did on screen.

The 1970s vogue for high-tech design accompanied the first wave of New York loft conversions, in which some of the city's grittiest industrial spaces were reclaimed for residential use. Early in our marriage, Jim and I moved into a vast loft in a former printing works on Murray Street in what is now TriBeCa. Back then it was a no man's land; herds of rats were our neighbors. When Jim and I split up, I decided to divide the loft in two, live in one half, and rent out the other. Richard Fiore, a handsome Italian-American builder, helped me with the work, the beginning of a business and personal relationship that led to our marriage in 1983.

Before that, however, Richard and I pooled our resources and bought the entire top floor of a commercial building on West 29th Street—a 3,300-square-foot space with 29 large, double-hung windows on four sides—which we converted into three apartments: one for Richard and his children; one for me; and one for Joseph Lembo. I was the designer (it was the first real project I did after graduating) and Richard was the builder. Devising a satisfactory layout was a big architectural challenge, but I reveled in it, and still think the resulting interiors were some of the best work I've done—especially my own 1,200-square-foot apartment. Since it was the one space over which I also had full decorative control, I could put all the principles I had learned from D'Urso into effect, and create a pure example of high-tech minimalism. It's not necessarily the way I would want to live now—too austere and hard-edged—but it was an authentic expression of the times.

The 14-month-long project was just the first in a string of residential conversions Richard and I have done since, as more and more of the city's formerly commercial neighborhoods gentrify. Chief among these has been the Meatpacking District, an area Lembo-Bohn helped pioneer when we opened our studio there in 1980. Back then, the area was curb-to-curb meat-processing plants; even Florent, the legendary all-night diner-*cum*-bistro, didn't arrive until 1985. We rented a little triangular building on Gansevoort Street. It was an empty wreck—along with constructing all the interiors, we had to put in windows and a roof—but charming and inexpensive. We would work from there happily for the next 16 years.

In 1996, Lembo-Bohn came to a sudden end. Thanks in part to our pioneering efforts, neighborhood rents shot up astronomically, ours included. At the same time, we were faced with meritless but potentially ruinous litigation, and our lawyer advised closing the business as the safest defensive strategy. We vacated our delightful little building; Joseph went to work for Ralph Lauren; and I set up my own firm, Laura Bohn Design Associates, which I run to this day.

I'm very proud of our work at Lembo-Bohn. (Ironically, we were inducted into the *Interior Design* Hall of Fame two years after the firm closed.) But I feel that the many projects I've done since are a more fully realized expression of my design sensibility. They are what I have chosen to feature in this book, and I think you will see why, unlike Billy Baldwin, I have always thought of myself as a "designer" and not a "decorator." My love of gray, which I use in almost every interior shown in these pages, best captures what I mean by that.

I have always been drawn back to gray as the predominant tonality in my spaces because, like the shadows on the facade of a building, it can articulate a piece of architecture, bring it to thrilling life, without drawing attention to itself. There's nothing wrong with wanting the color of an interior to be assertive and memorable, to paint it deep crimson and call it the Red Room. That's a traditional and legitimate way to think about decorating, but it's not what I'm interested in. I want you to experience and remember the integrated space—the full ensemble of furniture and art, arranged within a pleasingly defined, easily navigated volume—not to notice the striking shade of its walls.

Many designers use pure white for the same reasons, but I find it too stark and unrelenting—almost like being under a desert sun with no shade. Gray, on the other hand, is a wonderful chameleon that always seems to be changing its skin tone to blend in better. Using it, I have been able to temper the puritanism of D'Urso's modernism with the warmer, more forgiving sensuousness of Saladino's classicism. I think *Interior Design* recognized exactly what I have been doing when it dubbed me the "Queen of Soft Modern." In other words, I have found my own way of seeing. □

# CITY

*For me, designing in the city is about the architecture of transformation and renewal—of seeing the potential for evolution in its vast array of buildings, old and new. By reimagining the functional and aesthetic possibilities of existing urban spaces, I aim to give them a fresh sense of life.*

**THE MEATPACKING DISTRICT** A neighborhood that runs from Manhattan's West 14th Street south to Gansevoort Street, and from Eighth Avenue west to the Hudson River, the Meatpacking District was an almost comically sinister place when Joseph Lembo and I moved our firm there in 1980. Its streets, many paved with cobblestone-like Belgian blocks, ran with blood and grease from the numerous meat-processing plants. People avoided the area during the day because of the often-overpowering stench that emanated from the brick warehouses. In the middle of the night, butchers in blood-stained aprons would open the gates of their storefront businesses and unload dripping carcasses from enormous refrigerated trucks. The only other nocturnal street life was transvestite prostitutes looking for drive-by customers, drug dealers looking for the same, and gay men walking to the waterfront bars and underground clubs, many of them Mafia-controlled.

Friends and colleagues thought we were crazy to set up shop in such a Dantesque locale, but it had one huge advantage for a penniless startup like ours: The rents were very affordable. We found a little single-story building on the triangle between Gansevoort, West 13th, and Hudson streets. It was an empty wreck. Not only did the interior need to be completely reconstructed, but the roof and windows had to be replaced, too. Joseph and I did the redesign, and Richard did the construction. At first, we were too broke to afford proper furniture, let alone an adequate heating or air-conditioning system.

A neighboring meatpacker, seeing ice form on the inside of our windows, took pity on our semi-frozen state and lent us an industrial-strength overhead heater to get us through the first winter. But we loved our new home.

During the 16 years Lembo-Bohn maintained its triangular perch on Gansevoort, the neighborhood changed surprisingly little. Five years after we put down roots, Florent Morellet, a Parisian-émigré restaurateur, took over an all-night diner down the street, put a small pink-neon sign reading "florent" in the window, and began serving French bistro fare. It attracted a diverse clientele of artists, performers, and assorted nighthawks, who lent it a low-key, louche glamour. But even after it was joined by a smattering of bars, restaurants, and galleries, the area remained stubbornly grungy. As late as the mid-1990s, I had a young assistant return from lunch at Florent in hysterics, having almost tripped over a bloody horse's head lying in the snow. All that would change—and quite dramatically—but not for at least another five years. Gentrification in the Meatpacking District was taking its time.

PREVIOUS PAGES: MY DOGS AND I WERE PHOTOGRAPHED IN THE SUNKEN LIVING AREA OF OUR GROUND FLOOR LOFT APARTMENT IN THE CONVERTED NEW YORK COUNTY BANK BUILDING, WHICH WAS BUILT IN 1907. ABOVE LEFT: WE PURCHASED THE BANK BUILDING COMPLETE WITH ITS ORIGINAL SAFE. IT REMAINS A FOCAL POINT IN THE BUILDING LOBBY. LEFT: A CREW RIPS THE ROOF OFF THE BANK BUILDING BEFORE FRAMING THE PENTHOUSE ADDITION. OPPOSITE: THE BANK BUILDING LOCATED AT EIGHTH AVENUE AND 14TH STREET IN MANHATTAN HAD SAT EMPTY FOR YEARS BEFORE WE ACQUIRED IT. EARLY ON, I SKETCHED MY VISION FOR THE RENOVATION AND ADDITION.

## THE BANK BUILDING

Walking to work each day, I would pass a small but beautiful Beaux-Arts bank building on the southwest corner of Eighth Avenue and 14th Street. Designed by the New York–based firm of De Lemos & Cordes, the architects of the Macy's department store on 34th Street, and opened in 1907 as the New York County Bank Building, it is a superb little neo-classical temple with a limestone facade, bays of arched windows, and an imposing portico with Corinthian columns and a spread-winged eagle on the pediment. (It stands across the street from another marble temple—the former New York Savings Bank, built in 1897—to form, as *The A.I.A. Guide to New York City* explains, "a pair of classically inspired sentinels guarding the western corridor of 14th Street" leading to the Meatpacking District.) Closed as a bank in 1994, its massive 60-foot-high banking chamber stripped of every fitting and fixture, the landmarked building stood empty and derelict for two years until Richard and I decided to buy and convert it into condominium apartments.

Our plan for the bank building was greeted with the same incredulity as Lembo-Bohn's long-ago move to Gansevoort Street. It was a huge gamble that no other developer had been willing to take. Working on an historical structure of this type is always an architectural and financial challenge; when it is also located in a dubious neighborhood, the proposition becomes doubly unattractive. By this time, Richard and I had worked together on seven renovations, starting with the TriBeCa loft I was living in when we first met. We were on a roll and, looking at this as just one more residential conversion—writ much larger, of course—we decided to plunge in. I would work on the design with John Reimnitz and Lee Harris, New York–based architects with whom we often collaborated, and Richard would take care of the construction. The formula seemed to work.

Carving the massive volume into loft-style apartments was a process of torture followed by triumph. We must have done a thousand drawings to arrive at a coherent plan that gave us 11 units, all but one with its own outdoor space. The exterior of the landmarked building could not be altered, but almost nothing of the original interior remained, except the massive steel vault with its three-foot-thick doors, which we moved from the basement to the lobby as a decorative reminder that this was once a bank. We had to remove the roof to construct the five new floors of duplexes and triplexes, which were laid out to take full advantage of the enormous arched windows that overlooked 14th Street. On the top, we built a spectacular

ABOVE AND OPPOSITE: THE VAST, 60-FOOT-HIGH MAIN BANKING CHAMBER WAS COMPLETELY GUTTED.

steel-and-glass duplex penthouse, carefully set back on a wraparound terrace so that, as stipulated by the City Landmarks Commission, the addition is largely hidden from the street by the building's elaborate limestone parapets.

It took three years to complete the conversion, but selling the apartments took a lot longer. We deliberately left the individual apartments raw so that buyers could configure the large, high-ceilinged spaces for themselves. The glamour of the Beaux-Arts exterior and the size of the individual condominiums attracted a slew of well-heeled apartment seekers, including such celebrities as Meg Ryan, Kate Winslet, P. Diddy, and Scott Rudin. But to our dismay, there were no takers. Either they couldn't see past the units' sheetrock and concrete surfaces, and visualize the empty shells transformed into superb lofts, or they weren't ready to move to a neighborhood that in 1999 was still far from chic.

Richard and I moved into the penthouse and waited for buyers to recognize the potential of both the unfinished spaces and the ugly-duckling Meatpacking District. Slowly, units began to sell, mainly to investors who used them as pieds-à-terre. When the penthouse eventually sold, we moved into the ground-floor unit, a loft with 15-foot ceilings and an enormous back garden that we couldn't have given away in the beginning. All those prescient buyers would earn a big return on their investments. After 9/11, the area began to change with breathtaking speed. Designer boutiques, fancy eateries, and hip hotels seemed to spring up overnight. The repurposing of a disused elevated railroad track into the High Line park, which began in 2006, tied a lush green bow on the district's phenomenal turnaround.

**THE PENTHOUSE** Naturally, Richard and I were the first residents in the converted Bank Building, occupying the steel-and-glass duplex penthouse, a 3,000-square-foot addition I designed with architect Lee Harris. We had to lower the bank roof by about six feet so that the 27-foot-high structure would not become visually obtrusive. I gave it a traditional pitched roof of standing-seam metal, a detail that not only echoes the copper dome on the bank building across the street, but recalls the rural architecture of my native Texas.

As many visitors noted, the vast expanse of glazing made our pavilion home resemble a greenhouse—an effect only intensified by the potted trees and shrubs clustered on the wraparound terrace. I'm sure my engineer father would have disapproved of the soaring curtain walls as not being very energy-efficient, but the sheer pleasure of sitting in front of the living room's wood-burning fireplace—another environmental no-no—watching rain falling on the foliage outside helped assuage a lot of eco-guilt.

I hate to cut up space if I can avoid it, so the living room, dining room, kitchen, and library/guest room, which are all on the lower level, flow smoothly into one another. The monumental living room, which has a 20-foot-high ceiling, is approached through the more conventionally proportioned dining area. A partition wall partly blocks the view into the bigger room, so when visitors enter, its vast dimensions come as something of a surprise—an old trick that works every time. I specified poured terrazzo flooring throughout this level. It was more expensive than tile but it not only avoided having to level the uneven substrate, but also allowed me to custom-blend the colors, moving from a dark shade in the living room to a lighter one in the kitchen.

The second floor—a mezzanine overlooking the living room and terrace—housed the master suite and a small study. I was particularly pleased with the bathroom, which had a free-standing tub in front of glass doors opening onto a small planted terrace. When they were thrown back, it felt like you were bathing in the great outdoors—a delectable experience, especially given the thoroughly urban location.

PREVIOUS PAGES LEFT: THE NEO-CLASSICAL BANK BUILDING'S IMPOSING EIGHTH AVENUE PORTICO FEATURES CORINTHIAN COLUMNS AND A SPREAD-WINGED EAGLE ON THE PEDIMENT. RIGHT: THE LIVING ROOM'S INDUSTRIAL WINDOWS LOOK ONTO THE BUILDING'S ORIGINAL LIMESTONE BALUSTRADE. RICHARD AND I HAD TERRAZZO FLOORS POURED THROUGHOUT THE DUPLEX'S LOWER LEVEL.

Mark Rothko
Robert Rauschenberg

OPPOSITE: LASER-CUT STEEL FRAMES THE WORKING FIREPLACE IN THE LIVING ROOM, WHICH HAS A SECOND, FAUX FLUE BECAUSE I PREFER TO HAVE THEM IN PAIRS. A SITTING ROOM AND OFFICE ARE ON THE SECOND LEVEL. ABOVE: IN THE KITCHEN, I MIXED STAINLESS STEEL AND RIBBED WOOD.

PREVIOUS PAGES: FOR THE RIBBON-LIKE STAIRS, I WAS INSPIRED BY THE ONES IN THE NEW YORK CITY SUBWAY, WHICH HAVE A REVEAL BETWEEN THE STEPS AND THE WALL. THE ADJACENT DINING ROOM OPENS OUT TO A TERRACE. ABOVE: THE POURED CONCRETE COLUMNS IN THE GUEST ROOM WERE LEFT IN A RAW STATE. OPPOSITE: THE BATHROOM OPENS ONTO A PRIVATE PLANTED TERRACE.

OPPOSITE: AN EXTERIOR STAIR CONNECTS THE TWO LEVELS OF TERRACES.

BELOW: THE PENTHOUSE IS IDEAL FOR OUTDOOR SUMMER LIVING.

**THE LOFT** When a German businessman offered to rent our penthouse for an extraordinarily large amount of money, Richard and I moved into the last empty apartment in the building—2,700 square feet of raw space on the ground floor, with 15-foot-high ceilings, an inconvenient and ugly T-column at its center, and two courtyards, one quite large, the other small and internal. An awkward space that about 60 people had looked at without one offer having been made, it needed carefully considered planning.

As with the penthouse, I wanted as much flowing space as possible, so I created an enormous living-dining-kitchen area with a glass wall opening onto the larger courtyard, an attractive garden of gravel, pavers, and potted shrubs. I raised the kitchen/dining area floor a couple of feet, creating a sunken living area that was partly surrounded by broad wooden steps that can be used for seating. Years of paint had to be stripped off the living area's concrete floor that, once polished, took on the appearance of burnished leather—a gorgeous effect I happily take credit for, though it happened purely by chance.

I dealt with the pesky T-column by encasing it in a large cylinder of corrugated metallic plastic, turning an obvious eyesore into an architectural feature that not only helped direct the flow of space through the kitchen/dining area into the living area and garden courtyard beyond, but also provided convenient hidden storage. In addition, the new design feature supported a big flat-screen television that could be rotated to face either the living or dining areas. Paradoxically, the large, gleaming tube was considerably less intrusive than the smaller T-column underneath had been. By emphasizing rather than trying to disguise a design flaw, I made it appear and function as a fully intended architectural element in the overall plan.

PAGE 48: THE LOFT'S LUSH GARDEN COURTYARD GIVES THE ADJACENT LIVING ROOM THE FEEL OF A GREENHOUSE. PREVIOUS PAGES: THE SUNKEN LIVING AREA IS PARTLY SURROUNDED BY BROAD WOODEN STEPS THAT CAN BE USED FOR EXTRA SEATING. OPPOSITE: A LEDGE IN THE DEN AREA HOLDS A DISPLAY OF BLACK-AND-WHITE IMAGES BY AMERICAN PHOTOGRAPHER GORDON PARKS, AND SNAPSHOTS OF MY FAMILY. BELOW: BOTH THE LIVING AREA AND DEN HAVE SOFAS UPHOLSTERED IN A MIX OF FABRICS, AND FESTOONED WITH THROW PILLOWS.

PREVIOUS PAGES: A LARGE CYLINDER OF CORRUGATED METALLIC PLASTIC SHEATHES AN AWKWARDLY PLACED STRUCTURAL COLUMN NEAR THE DINING AREA. RIGHT: IN THE OPEN KITCHEN, I SPECIFIED SEVERAL SURFACE FINISHES, INCLUDING GLASS, LACQUER, WOOD, AND STAINLESS STEEL. OVERLEAF: A SPIRAL STAIR LEADS TO THE SECOND-LEVEL LOFT SPACE.

*Carving the bank building's massive interior volume into loft-style apartments was a process of torture followed by triumph. We must have done 1,000 drawings to arrive at a coherent plan that gave us 11 units, each but one with its own outdoor space.*

RIGHT: THE MASTER BATHROOM HAS A PORCELAIN TILE RADIANT-HEATED FLOOR AND WALLS PAINTED IN SHERWIN-WILLIAMS' AQUA-VELVET, A PALE, PALE GREENISH BLUE I LIKE TO USE A LOT. A CUSTOM-MADE SLATTED ALUMINUM TABLE SUPPORTS THE SINK.

## UPPER WEST SIDE

There is no greater pleasure for a designer than working with a fully engaged client. This project—a city pied-à-terre for a Scarsdale, New York–based family—whose classic beach house on the Rockaway peninsula I had previously designed—began as a kitchen makeover but grew into a two-year gut renovation thanks to the owners' boundless enthusiasm. They bought an apartment on Manhattan's Central Park West after falling for the 1930 building's Art Deco style, particularly its Streamline Moderne lobby, an elegant space that could double as the sleek setting for a Fred Astaire and Ginger Rogers dance number. Its classic Art Deco motifs included acres of polished marble, bronze ribbing on the walls, etched glass panels, and chrome-plated fixtures. The family wanted some of that giddy 1930s glamour in their new home.

The three-bedroom apartment's period interiors were a dark and dreary warren of small spaces, well beyond the point of restoration. So, with my clients' encouragement, I recreated the lobby's iconic style in the apartment not by slavishly reproducing its decorative elements but by freely reimagining them in contemporary terms. We did go down and measure all the Deco detailing, however, so that we would get the underlying relationships of scale and proportion right. This paid off when designing a ribbed wall that angles its way from the entry to the kitchen, as it did when getting the fluting on a white plaster column just right, so that it evokes jazz-age chic rather than classical solemnity.

We kept the color palette light, airy, and subtle—there are three shades of pale-gray paint in a pearly eggshell finish in the living room alone—with metallic touches adding a little shimmer and dazzle: gold, brass, and bronze furniture in the living room; stainless-and-leather dining chairs; and silver paint rubbed into the oak floors to give them a soft glow. Nickel-plated fittings gleam in the master bathroom, the apartment's most overtly Streamline Moderne space. The lobby's bronze ribbing is echoed by horizontal stripes of brown porcelain tile on the creamy marble walls, while the Art Deco-inspired fixtures and the glittery jewel-like mouth-blown glass chandelier overhead raise the room's glamour quotient by several notches.

PREVIOUS PAGES LEFT: A CURTAIN SEPARATES THE KITCHEN FROM THE DINING AREA IN THIS COMPLETELY RENOVATED ART DECO-ERA APARTMENT. ABOVE AND RIGHT: I FURNISHED THE LIVING ROOM WITH GOLD LEATHER UPHOLSTERY, A RUG IN A SWIRLY METALLIC PATTERN, AND GOLD AND BLUE PAINTINGS COMMISSIONED FROM THE POLISH-AMERICAN ARTIST STASZEK KOTOWSKI. OVERLEAF LEFT AND RIGHT: THE HALLWAY'S RIBBED WALLS WERE INSPIRED BY THE BUILDING'S ART DECO LOBBY.

OPPOSITE: A SOFA SWIVELS INTO A QUEEN-SIZE BED TO ACCOMMODATE OVERNIGHT GUESTS. THE SPACE DOUBLES AS A PLAYROOM, COMPLETE WITH EERO AARNIO PUPPIES TO AMUSE THE CHILDREN. BELOW: IN THE MASTER BEDROOM, A CUSTOM-MADE ANTIQUED MIRROR ON THE WALL BEHIND THE DECO-STYLE BED FUNCTIONS MORE LIKE A WINDOW THAN A LOOKING GLASS. OVERLEAF LEFT AND RIGHT: THE GLAMOROUS BATHROOM IS COMPLETELY ART DECO-INSPIRED. IT FEATURES BOOK-MATCHED MARBLE THROUGHOUT, LEFROY BROOKS HARDWARE, AND A GLASS DOOR THAT OPERATES BOTH AS A SHOWER SCREEN AND AN ENTRYWAY.

**GREENWICH VILLAGE** Lack of adequate natural light is a common problem in New York apartments. But this 1,500-square-foot, three-bedroom loft in Greenwich Village was beyond gloomy. It was a bat cave. The layout was also depressing, with a space-hogging kitchen dominating the living area, and a minuscule bathroom next to an oversized dressing room in the master suite. I had some leeway in tackling those problems since the owners mostly used the place for theater-going weekends in the city. While the kitchen could be minimized—they dined out a lot—there needed to be sufficient sleeping and bathroom facilities to accommodate frequent overnight guests.

I gutted the place, created a 40-foot-long living-dining-kitchen area, enlarged the existing bathroom—and added another. There was no way to bring in more daylight, so I installed die-cut curtains over all the windows and, by backlighting them, created the illusion of sunlight streaming through the lacy floor-to-ceiling fabric. Further illumination is supplied by overhead track lighting, numerous floor and table lamps, and a row of upward-pointing sconces. These run the full length of the living-area, whose walls and ceiling are finished in glossy paint—a rarity for me—to help bounce the light around even more. At the sconce level, about two-thirds of the way up the wall, the paint color changes from pale-gray to white, which creates a dome-like sense of light and space overhead.

The kitchen, which is tucked into a corner, comprises two adjoining walls of white cabinetry with gleaming stainless-steel appliances, hardware, and baseboards. When the kitchen is not in use, a free-standing aluminum screen can be drawn across to conceal it from the main living area. Near the kitchen, what appears to be a column of tightly wound rope rises to the ceiling. It is actually a downpipe that could not be moved, so I hid it in plain sight by wrapping it in sparkly white cord. Blond bamboo flooring, white and beige mid-20th century modern furniture, and apple-green accents all help keep the environment bright and cheerful. The only dark element is the fireplace surround, which I had painted with blackboard paint so messages can be scrawled on it in chalk—a both playful and practical solution.

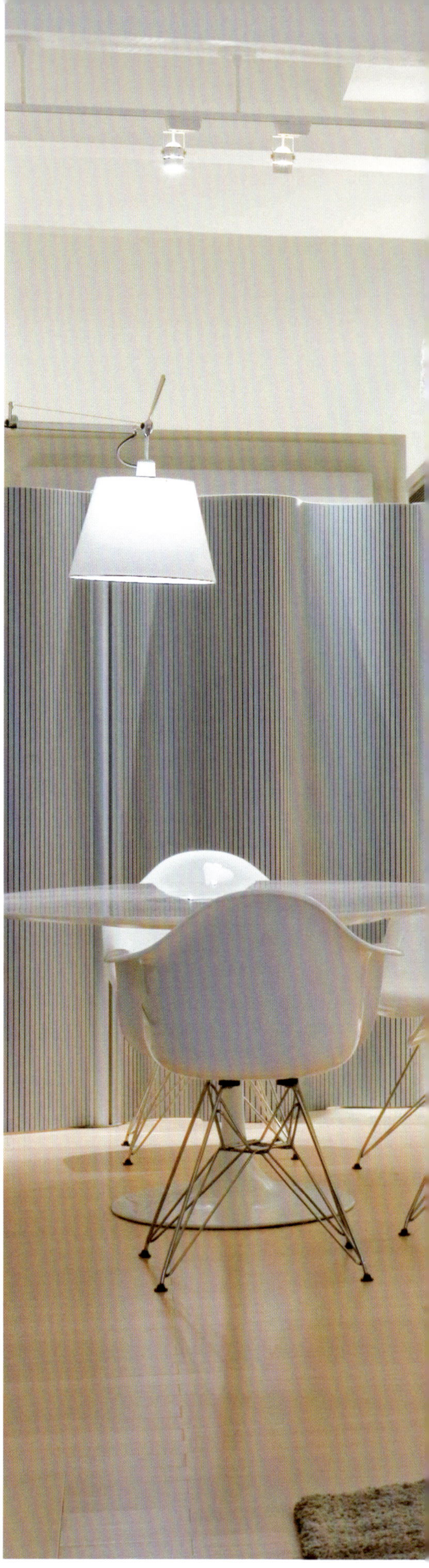

PREVIOUS PAGES LEFT: WE TRANSFORMED A PITCH-DARK PIED-À-TERRE INTO A BRIGHT CRASH PAD FOR TEN PEOPLE. THE BANQUETTE, WHICH ADDS COLOR AND TEXTURE, DOUBLES AS A BED. ABOVE AND RIGHT: I TIED THE LIVING ROOM TOGETHER BY PAINTING THE LOWER PORTION OF THE WALL GRAY AND THE UPPER PORTION WHITE. ITALIAN ARCHITECT MICHELE DE LUCCHI'S CLASSIC *TOLOMEO* ALUMINUM SCONCES ARE INSTALLED WHERE THE TWO COLORS MEET EACH OTHER.

PREVIOUS PAGES: THE VERTICAL RIBBED SCREEN, SOURCED FROM AN OFFICE FURNITURE CATALOG, IS MADE OF ALUMINUM ON ONE SIDE AND WOOD ON THE OTHER, WHILE AN EXISTING PIPE IS TURNED INTO A DECORATIVE ELEMENT BY WRAPPING IT IN TASSELED PLASTIC ROPE. ABOVE: I USED BLACKBOARD PAINT ON THE FIREPLACE SURROUND SO CHALK MESSAGES CAN BE WRITTEN ON IT. THE LIGHTING BEHIND THE CURTAINS IN EVERY ROOM MAKES THE SPACE ALWAYS APPEAR TO BE SUNNY. OPPOSITE: THE SECOND BATHROOM HAS A SINK INSTALLED ATOP A RESTAURANT SUPPLY CART.

RIGHT: AFTER SPRAYING A SKIM COAT OF GRAY PAINT ON THE BRICK WALL OF THE MASTER BEDROOM, I INSTALLED A HEADBOARD THAT INCORPORATES UPHOLSTERY AND WOOD.

# COUNTRY

*Like the city, the country offers countless opportunities to remake the built environment. But the beauty of the landscape and the long-breathed rhythms of rural life call for a gentler hand, one that provides for modern living yet honors nature and tradition.*

**BUCKS COUNTY** In the early 1980s, a client invited Richard and me to spend a few days at her weekend house in Bucks County, Pennsylvania, an unspoiled stretch of country along the Delaware River. Even though it is only a three-hour drive from Manhattan, we had never visited the area before, and we fell instantly in love. While the county is named after Buckinghamshire in England, its rolling hills and broad vistas reminded me of Tuscany, Italy. The vernacular architecture—covered bridges, stone barns, quaint little towns that retain a pre-Industrial Revolution charm, and lots of 17th and 18th century Quaker houses, many made with the iconic local fieldstone—however, is very American. Less expensive and buttoned-up than Connecticut, Westchester, Long Island, and the other traditional rural bolt-holes, 1930s Bucks County became a hotbed of transplanted Manhattan cultural talent—lyricist Oscar Hammerstein, playwrights Moss Hart and George S. Kaufman, humorist S.J. Perelman, and novelist Nathanael West among them—that it became known as "The Genius Belt."

On that first weekend visit, Richard and I found a property that we subsequently bought. A charming 18th-century stone building on a river, it had once been a mill but was now a thoroughly decrepit three-bedroom house. It took us two years of backbreaking, if rewarding, toil to renovate the little place. It would be just the first of five properties we have owned and transformed in Bucks County so far. Renovating this succession of rural houses and barns, which ranged in age from the 1730s to the 1950s, and included a 1930s mail order kit house from the Sears, Roebuck *Modern Homes* catalog, has allowed me to explore an even broader array of architectural styles, periods, and traditions than our urban projects. Each one has involved a lot of research, some of it in local libraries and archives, poring through deeds and documents written in sepia ink.

Bucks County has also let us indulge our other passion: rescuing abandoned animals. This goes well beyond dogs and cats to include peacocks, guinea hens, goats, horses, and other large critters that will soon include, I hope, a llama or two. Our most recent draftees were a pair of miniature horses that were about to be evicted from a nearby farm. At first, naively, we treated these beautiful little creatures like overgrown house pets, giving them free run of the kitchen or walking them down the road on leashes. It took a few alarming incidents to wake us to the fact that these tiny charmers were 200-pound powerhouses that could pull us around effortlessly if they had a mind to. So now, we live in the house and they live in the barn.

## OTTSVILLE 1

Our current house, in Ottsville, is the most completely transformative Bucks County project we have done so far. A crumbling 1950s brick ruin when we bought it in 2000, it was home to the same farmer who had sold us the adjacent 19th-century property we were living in back then. In fact, the two houses, although some distance apart, stood on what had been a single dairy farm. The farmer had built the ranch house with his own hands, but had let it fall into complete disrepair as he aged and eventually died. When we saw the "For Sale" sign, the prospect of restoring a house not too dissimilar to the one my father had designed for us long ago in Texas—even if this one was a total wreck—was more than Richard and I could resist.

Yet again, our family and friends thought we were delusional in taking on such a Sisyphean task. In the end, we had little choice but to tear most of the derelict structure down to its concrete-slab foundation, and built it back up from there. While expanding the footprint to 4,000 square feet, we also excavated by four feet, thereby allowing enough height for larger, view-friendly windows. The exterior is a collection of low-slung clapboard volumes with an aluminum roofline that changes level no fewer than 13 times, as does the floor plate inside. This gave rise to all sorts of complex intersecting geometries, which readily tested my planning acumen and Richard's building skills to the limit.

The interior has some industrial touches that recall my training with Joseph D'Urso. Many of the larger, pitched-roof spaces are spanned by steel-rod ties, complete with turnbuckles, in place of the more traditional timber rafters. The materials we chose included unfinished metals and exposed concrete. But there is a lot of wood, too—mahogany planks, salvaged from a football stadium, panel the den; a row of tree trunks, *au naturel*, forms a floor-to-ceiling divider between the living and dining areas; and there are many pieces of wooden furniture, including a custom bed in walnut, driftwood side tables, vintage finds from pine chests to oak cabinets.

PAGES 82-83: ME IN THE SLEEK KITCHEN OF MY COUNTRY HOUSE IN OTTSVILLE, PENNSYLVANIA, THE FIFTH PROPERTY I'VE RENOVATED IN BUCKS COUNTY. PREVIOUS PAGES LEFT: BAILEY LIKES RESTING ON THE EAMES LOUNGE CHAIR IN THE KITCHEN. A WOODEN CANOE IS DISPLAYED IN THE NICHE ABOVE. LEFT: WE COMPLETELY RENOVATED THE DERELICT 1950s HOUSE, LOCATED ON OUR BUCOLIC BUCKS COUNTY PROPERTY, WHICH WAS MORE A FALL-DOWN THAN A TEAR-DOWN.

ABOVE AND RIGHT: SLATTED WALLS ON THE SCREENED PORCH ARE INSPIRED BY MY MEMORY OF A STRIPPED-DOWN BARN NEARBY. FOLLOWING DESIGNER JOSEPH D'URSO'S EMPHASIS ON CREATING FOCUS, I DESIGNED WINDOWS CENTERED ON THE VIEW.

lemon
salsa
pickles

PREVIOUS PAGES AND LEFT: TO ME, THE KITCHEN IS THE BEST ROOM IN THE HOUSE AND, MEASURING 37 FEET BY 23 FEET, ALSO THE LARGEST. THE FLOOR, PAVED WITH LOCAL SLATE, HAS THREE DRAINS THAT ALLOW IT TO BE HOSED DOWN WITHOUT FUSS. I SALVAGED THE GIANT LIGHT FIXTURES FROM A NEIGHBOR'S DUSTY BARN. ABOVE: AN OIL PAINTING BY AMERICAN ARTIST DAVID SEAR HANGS IN ONE CORNER.

OPPOSITE AND BELOW: WHEN A NEIGHBOR WAS CUTTING TREE TRUNKS, WE CARRIED HOME THOSE WE COULD TO USE AS A DIVIDER BETWEEN THE LIVING AND DINING AREAS. OVERLEAF RIGHT: THE WORKING FIREPLACE ON THE DINING ROOM WALL IS RAISED BECAUSE WE LOWERED THE FLOOR BY TWO FEET DURING THE RENOVATION BUT LEFT THE FIREPLACE AT ITS ORIGINAL LEVEL.

*The interior has industrial touches that recall my training with Joseph D'Urso. Pitched-roof spaces are spanned by steel-rod ties, complete with turnbuckles, in place of traditional timber rafters. Materials included unfinished metals and exposed concrete, but there is a lot of wood, too.*

ABOVE AND RIGHT: ORIGINALLY A WARREN OF DARK ROOMS WITH LOW CEILINGS, THE LIVING AREA IS NOW A DOUBLE-HEIGHT SPACE WITH PICTURE WINDOWS AND A MIX OF TEXTURES AND MATERIALS. OVERLEAF: THE RIBBED HALLWAY LEADING FROM THE LIVING AREA TO THE BEDROOMS EXPRESSES MY PREFERENCE FOR HORIZONTAL LINES.

PREVIOUS PAGES: I PAINTED THE PANELED POOL ROOM WALL IN PURPLISH-BLUE. PANELING CONCEALS A HIDDEN DOORWAY TO A CRAFTS ROOM. ABOVE: LULU SITS ON THE BED IN THE MASTER BEDROOM. OPPOSITE: A PAINTING BY THE BROOKLYN, NEW YORK ARTIST KATHRYN LYNCH DOMINATES THE ROOM.

PREVIOUS PAGES: AN ENORMOUS IMAGE OF MARILYN MONROE PRINTED ON VINYL WALLPAPER SERVES AS A GLAMOROUS MURAL IN THE MASTER BATHROOM. OPPOSITE AND ABOVE: THE POWDER-ROOM SINK IS MOUNTED IN A SLAB OF CHAIN-SAWED WOOD FROM THE LOCAL LUMBER YARD.

ABOVE AND OPPOSITE: THE HOUSE HAS 13 LEVEL CHANGES. WE RESTORED THE CHARMING FACADE OF OUR ANTIQUE BARN. OVERLEAF AND PAGES 114-115: THE ORIGINAL BARN WAS COMPLETELY REBUILT AND EXPANDED, INCLUDING THE ADDITION OF A DRAMATIC GLASS WALL OVERLOOKING THE PENNSYLVANIA FARMLAND.

## OTTSVILLE 2

After 15 years' living happily on our second property in Bucks County, a renovated 18th-century house and barn in Erwinna, Richard and I were lured away by a 50-acre farm in Ottsville, just a few miles down the road. We bought the place for the superb lay of land, the magnificent trees, and the extraordinary views. With no other buildings in sight anywhere, it was a setting of such arcadian beauty it made your head spin. The farmhouse, a small 19th-century brick structure on an older foundation, was in awful shape. It had been added to, over the years, and the rooms were tiny and dark. I thought of the traditional farmhouses in Tuscany, Italy, which were built with few windows so that the workers inside would not be distracted by the views of the glorious countryside.

I was determined that the house take advantage of the stunning vistas at every opportunity. We plastered the brick exterior with concrete stucco, gutted the interior down to the joists, and either added or enlarged windows wherever we could. In the living room, for example, a new floor-to-ceiling triple-casement window, set in a large alcove addition, offered a knockout view of the adjoining valley. In the master bathroom, a porthole installed in the shower wall overlooks horses grazing in the neighboring paddock. And removing part of the master bedroom ceiling exposed an attic window that lets moonlight dapple the bedroom floor.

Although the renovation left us with fewer but larger rooms, they were still not big, so I kept the furnishings simple and honest—a contemporary pedestal table and a handful of antique chairs pulled up to a pew-like upholstered bench defined the dining area. A pair of clean-lined modern sofas and a similarly unfussy vintage armchair and ottoman anchored the living room. There was nothing that would overwhelm the clean, compact spaces we had created. Unbelievably, there wasn't a single fireplace in the 100-year-old house. So we built a chimney with two back-to-back fireplaces—one in the living room, the other on the terrace. And we turned this broad, paved expanse into a true outdoor room by covering it with a simple wooden pergola. Furnished with a large round table, a few wrought-iron chairs, and a hip Philippe Starck plastic loveseat, it was the space we used the most, starting our day by having breakfast there, and closing it with a martini by the fire and under the stars.

PREVIOUS PAGES LEFT: RICHARD AND I CREATED A BUCOLIC TERRACE COMPLETE WITH A WORKING FIREPLACE WHERE THE 1950S-ERA KITCHEN ADDITION ONCE STOOD. ABOVE AND OPPOSITE: WE PURCHASED THE LAND BECAUSE THE BEAUTIFUL ROLLING HILLS REMINDED US OF THE TUSCAN COUNTRYSIDE IN ITALY. THE TINY BRICK HOUSE ON THE SITE WAS LONG NEGLECTED, COVERED IN BRAMBLES, AND SURROUNDED BY DEAD TREES. WE RE-SCULPTED THE LAND, PLASTERED THE FACADE, REPLACED THE DOORS AND WINDOWS, AND ADDED OUTDOOR LIVING SPACES.

ABOVE: THE VIGNETTE INCLUDES A 1930S SILVER-PLATED ROWING TROPHY TURNED INTO A LAMP, AND A BOX TO WHICH I GLUED SOME OF THE MANY BUTTONS I'VE COLLECTED OVER THE YEARS. OPPOSITE: THE ORIGINAL HOUSE WAS COMPLETELY GUTTED AND REWORKED. I REDESIGNED THE STAIR, MOVED THE ENTRY, PLASTERED THE WALLS IN A SAND COLOR, AND USED FURNISHINGS THAT FUNCTIONED IN A SMALL SPACE, INCLUDING A ONE-FOOT-DEEP SCHOOL BENCH IN THE DINING AREA.

PREVIOUS PAGES: IN THE TINY LIVING ROOM, BEYOND THE DINING AREA, I ADDED FRINGE SKIRTING TO THE MODERN LEATHER SOFAS. ABOVE AND OPPOSITE: LOCATED IN THE ATTIC, BOTH MY OFFICE AND THE GUEST ROOM HAVE ROMANTIC PITCHED CEILINGS AND SKYLIGHTS. OVERLEAF LEFT AND RIGHT: WHEN I REPLACED THE ENTRY WITH A POWDER ROOM, I KEPT THE IVY FROM THE FRONT DOOR INTACT. A SINK WAS INSTALLED IN A RAW WOOD COUNTERTOP, AND A FOUND TREE BRANCH WAS USED TO HOLD THE TOILET PAPER.

**ERWINNA** The second of our five Bucks County properties, one we bought in 1985, was also the oldest and the largest: a five-bedroom Quaker house, parts of which dated back to the early 18th century, with an adjoining 19th-century barn, both built of stone. They sat on 70 acres of land that included a pair of wedding trees—gorgeous maples planted by a Quaker bride and groom more than 180 years ago. Located in Erwinna, the house was more recently part of "The Genius Belt," having been owned for the previous 50 years by a film producer who worked on *Gone with the Wind.* It was also near Fox Farm, the weekend house of writer Dorothy Parker and her husband, the actor and screenwriter Alan Campbell, during the 1930s and 1940s.

I worked with Joseph Lembo on the renovation. Because the house had grown over the years, the layout was very quirky, but in attractive and interesting ways. So we did not change the floor plan much beyond replacing the kitchen—a hideous 1940s extension that Richard literally sawed off the house and threw on a bonfire—with a beautiful light-filled version. We put the dining room in the oldest portion of the house, a large single room where family life would have taken place, including cooking and eating. It had an extraordinary wood-paneled wall that incorporated cupboards, doors, and an enormous walk-in fireplace with folding shutters. Behind one door lay a narrow staircase leading up to the original sleeping quarters under a peaked roof. The living room wing, added in the 1830s by the couple who planted the maples, had more bedrooms upstairs and two side-by-side front doors—one for men, one for women.

Most of our energy went into reversing 50 years of neglect. The movie-producer owner appeared to have done nothing to maintain the house beyond applying coat upon coat of paint—mostly in unpleasant shades of green—which we painstakingly stripped off. I was careful to ensure that none of the refinished surfaces looked shiny and new. The wood paneling in the dining room, for instance, was given an antique treatment because when it was cleaned up, it didn't appear old at all. And the plaster walls were repainted to give the impression they were slightly mildewed. Much of the flooring was original—wide planks of pumpkin pine, a once-plentiful and inexpensive wood that is now rare and highly prized for the glorious patina it acquires over time. The restored boards brought an almost flamboyant beauty to the otherwise restrained Quaker interiors. We delighted in the restoration.

PREVIOUS PAGES LEFT: I LOVE THE DINING ROOM'S ORIGINAL LATE-18TH-CENTURY WOOD PANELING AND SHUTTERED FIREPLACE. LEFT: THAT THE 18TH-CENTURY HOUSE WAS BUILT BY QUAKERS, WHO SEPARATED THE SEXES, IS REFLECTED IN THE DINING ROOM'S TWIN DOORS: ONE FOR MEN AND ONE FOR WOMEN. I ACQUIRED THE LARGE SHAKER CUPBOARD AT AN AUCTION; THE DINING TABLE AND THE IRONWORK CHANDELIER ARE MY OWN DESIGN.

PREVIOUS PAGES: A 12-FOOT-LONG BANQUETTE COVERED IN PILLOWS AND AN ANTIQUE TABLE WITH CLEAN MODERN LINES ARE IN THE NEWLY ADDED KITCHEN. LEFT: THE MASTER BEDROOM'S MOLDINGS AND DRAPERIES ARE MORE TRADITIONAL THAN MY USUAL STYLE. I PAINTED THE ROOM AN INTENSE SHADE OF PURPLE AND THEN APPLIED A LAYER OF WHITEWASH TO TONE IT DOWN.

WATER

## ROCKAWAY PARK

Astonishingly, this beach house—my first of several projects for a delightful Scarsdale, New York-based family—is located within New York City, on the Rockaway Peninsula, an 11-mile sliver of land on the south shore of Queens. But with its sandy beaches, grassy dunes, and small-town mien, the oceanside neighborhood feels more Cape Cod than Big Apple. The 1930s two-story vacation house my clients bought did not share the area's resort-like vibe. Dark and poorly laid out, it needed a complete gut renovation. So I set out to transform the place into something appropriately bright and breezy.

By moving the entrance, we turned the outmoded kitchen into an expansive foyer with slate floor tile and white-lacquered beadboard wainscoting. This classic beach house paneling extends from the foyer into the new kitchen, where a light maple floor, hand-rubbed ash cabinets, pale green quartz counters, and white ceramic tile backsplashes perpetuate the breezy mood. Meals are served at an elliptical limed-ash table that swings out for easy access. If the table's generous banquette looks ready to seat a small army, that's because the 7,000-square-foot house is designed to accommodate up to 24 grandchildren.

There's room for everyone at the 14-foot-long teak table in the dining room, too. The living room, designed as a cozy parental retreat, shares the dining room's light maple floor and pale gray walls, but the two spaces are intelligently separated by a wall of glass doors that allows children to be seen but not heard. Most of the kids sleep in an attic dormitory, where upholstered window seats double as sleeping areas, and all the beds are on wheels so they can be moved around easily. I applied my signature half-and-half wall treatment to the attic spaces: In the bathroom, the lower portion of the walls are white tile, while the upper portions are painted yellow; the bedroom walls are pale green up to eye level and brilliant white above.

PREVIOUS PAGES LEFT: BUILT IN THE 1930S, THE TRADITIONAL CLAPBOARD BEACH HOUSE'S DARK AND POKEY INTERIOR NEEDED A GUT RENOVATION. ABOVE AND OPPOSITE: I TURNED THE LIVING ROOM INTO A COZY PARENTAL RETREAT BY SURROUNDING IT WITH GLASS WALLS THAT ALLOW CHILDREN TO BE SEEN BUT NOT HEARD. THE BREEZY DINING ROOM HAS BUILT-IN STORAGE AND A 14-FOOT-LONG CUSTOM TABLE—A NECESSITY IN A HOUSE THAT MUST ACCOMMODATE UP TO 24 GRANDCHILDREN AT MEALTIMES.

OPPOSITE: WITH KIDS IN MIND, I CREATED A LOW-MAINTENANCE BATHROOM WITH BIG ROUND MIRRORS AND LOTS OF HOOKS FOR WET TOWELS AND BATHING SUITS. BELOW: THE ONCE-DERELICT ATTIC NOW SLEEPS UP TO EIGHT KIDS DORMITORY-STYLE. THE ROLLING BEDS AND BUILT-IN BANQUETTE MAKE THE SPACE ADAPTABLE.

**THE HAMPTONS** I made full use of texture and color in designing this new two-story beach house, which was huge: seven bedrooms, 12 bathrooms, a vast kitchen, a gym, and more. There's a lot of gray and a lot of wood, but juxtaposed with brilliant white to keep the interiors light and beach-like in feeling. In the dining room, walnut establishes the overall tonality—dark-espresso walnut chairs, a lighter walnut table, and a medium-dark walnut floor—but the space feels fresh and breezy thanks to the surface textures: pale gray walls in a low-luster eggshell finish that has a slight sheen, which lends them a degree of animation they would lack if the paint were totally flat; a ceiling painted bright white in a satin finish that also reflects the light, giving the dining room a little sparkle, as does the high-gloss lacquer on the sideboard.

In the kitchen, I specified walnut for the floor and the island, but finished the latter in a lighter stain so that it stands out like a separate piece of furniture. The rest of the space is a serene composition of soft, subtle colors. The walls are a pale gray and the cabinets are in a soothing putty tone rather than pure white, which would have been too severe. The kitchen gets a lot of light, so the cabinetry also needed to be a soothing color. Marble adds to the sense of calm: I used a lightly figured Carrara marble for the backsplash and a more boldly patterned Calacatta marble for the countertop on the island, because that element is the natural focus of the room.

PREVIOUS PAGES LEFT AND LEFT: IN THE LIVING ROOM OF THIS RAMBLING WEEKEND HOME FOR A FAMILY WITH THREE GROWN CHILDREN, I USED SEVERAL PALE COLORS TOGETHER FOR THE FURNISHINGS AND WALLS TO CREATE A RELAXED SETTING. OVERLEAF RIGHT: IN THE DINING ROOM, WALNUT ESTABLISHES THE OVERALL TONALITY—DARK-ESPRESSO WALNUT CHAIRS, A LIGHTER WALNUT TABLE, AND A MEDIUM-DARK WALNUT FLOOR—BUT THE SPACE FEELS FRESH AND BREEZY THANKS TO PALE-GRAY EGGSHELL WALLS, A SATIN-FINISH CEILING IN BRIGHT WHITE, AND A HIGH-GLOSS LACQUERED SIDEBOARD.

*I made full use of texture and color in designing this new two-story beach house, which was huge: seven bedrooms, 12 bathrooms, a vast kitchen, a gym, and more. There's a lot of gray and a lot of wood, but juxtaposed with brilliant white to keep the interiors light and airy in feeling.*

RIGHT: THE CLIENTS, WHO LIKE TO COOK, EAT, AND ENTERTAIN, WANTED A KITCHEN THAT ACCOMMODATED THEIR LIFESTYLE. I MAINTAINED A MUTED PALETTE FOR PAINT, UPHOLSTERY, AND WOOD FINISHES THROUGHOUT. OVERLEAF LEFT AND RIGHT: EACH HALLWAY IN THE THREE-STORY HOME IS DIFFERENTIATED BY THE USE OF NEW FLOORING MATERIAL, LIGHT FIXTURES, AND SHADES OF GRAY PAINT THAT VARY ON EVERY LEVEL. PAGES 152–153: THE BASEMENT GYM, MY FAVORITE ROOM IN THE HOUSE, INCLUDES A BOLD PHOTO-MURAL THAT SPANS TWO OF THE WALLS.

SPRI
SPRI

## MERCER ISLAND

I worked in close collaboration with Seattle–based SKB Architects on the renovation of this serene house on Mercer Island in Lake Washington, a leafy residential community that is part of metropolitan Seattle.

It was my fourth major project in 20 years for the clients, a bank executive, his wife, and family. They would move every three years or so, and had already called on me to design a penthouse in Manhattan, a house on the water in Connecticut, and a townhouse in England—each very different—before I tackled this house, which is also on the water. Our tastes have evolved in tandem through that period—getting more modern, but always retaining a soft, warm touch.

The Seattle house needed to incorporate the full warehouse of antique furniture they had acquired in England, so it's at the more traditional end of my design spectrum. We supplemented the period pieces with clean-lined contemporary furniture that keeps the look fresh and up-to-date. Although it was big, the existing house was not well-designed—many of the rooms were chopped up—so we ripped a lot of it apart to create large, airy, sun-filled interiors to accommodate the antiques and yet exude a modern sense of light, color, and space. We installed large expanses of glazing that take advantage of the spectacular views out to the lake from every window, bringing the beauty of the natural setting indoors.

PREVIOUS PAGES LEFT: I WORKED WITH THE SEATTLE, WASHINGTON-BASED SKB ARCHITECTS TO TRANSFORM THIS WONDERFUL OLD HOUSE ON MERCER ISLAND, WASHINGTON. LEFT: THE LIVING ROOM IS FURNISHED IN A MIX OF STYLES—EVERYTHING FROM MODERN PIECES FROM HOLLY HUNT TO TRADITIONAL ENGLISH ANTIQUES THAT THE CLIENT ALREADY OWNED. THE SISAL RUG WAS CUSTOM-MADE. OVERLEAF RIGHT: THE KITCHEN AFFORDS SPECTACULAR VIEWS OF LAKE WASHINGTON AND THE SURROUNDING WOODED LANDSCAPE.

*We ripped the house apart to create airy, sun-filled interiors that accommodate antiques yet exude a modern sense of light, color, and space. And we installed expanses of glass to take advantage of the spectacular views of the lake, bringing the beauty of the natural setting indoors.*

LEFT: LIKE THE REST OF THE HOUSE, THE DINING ROOM INCLUDES PIECES FROM THE EXTENSIVE COLLECTION OF ANTIQUES THE PERIPATETIC CLIENTS TAKE WITH THEM WHEREVER THEY MOVE. OVERLEAF RIGHT: IN THE MASTER BEDROOM, I CREATED A RECESSED WALL IN BLOND WOOD TO FRAME THE BED. PAGES 164–165: THE MASTER BATHROOM IS A SERENE COMPOSITION OF WOOD, STONE, AND IDYLLIC VIEWS.

## OLD SNOWMASS

Working with great modern architecture in a spectacular natural setting is any designer's idea of a good time. When the client is also a close friend, the job is pretty much bliss. Such was the case with this family retreat in Colorado's Elk Mountains. The architecture, by Larry Yaw of Cottle Carr Yaw Architects Ltd. in Basalt, Colorado, was a major influence on the interiors. The house, which is laid out superbly, with wonderful proportions and thoughtful details, is the opposite of the McMansions you often encounter in and around Aspen. It's not designed to knock your socks off, though it certainly does.

The architectural materials were natural, luxurious, and practical, so I took color and texture cues from them. All the furniture was selected for comfort—the client came with me to every showroom and sat in every chair before giving his approval—and kept low to the ground so as not to obstruct the fabulous alpine views. Fabrics ranged from mohair to velvet to soft, nubby tweed, all in neutral tones that go well with wood, stone, and other natural surfaces. Light fixtures, such as an arched floor lamp in the living area and a pendant with multiple drum shades over the dining table, were chosen for their sculptural qualities, while accessories and artworks were kept to a minimum so they didn't distract from the architecture or the scenery.

PREVIOUS PAGES LEFT: I FOUND THE SOPHISTICATED MODERNIST ARCHITECTURE OF THIS COLORADO MOUNTAIN RETREAT, DESIGNED BY LARRY YAW, OF THE BASALT, COLORADO, FIRM COTTLE CARR YAW ARCHITECTS, INSPIRING. RIGHT: GIVEN THE STRENGTH OF THE ARCHITECTURE AND SETTING, I KEPT THE LIVING ROOM VERY LOW-KEY, WITH COMFORTABLE FURNITURE IN MUTED COLORS, AND MY SIGNATURE MIX OF TONES AND TEXTURES. OVERLEAF LEFT AND RIGHT: THE ENTRY STAIRCASE LEADS UP TO THE LIVING ROOM, KITCHEN, AND FAMILY BEDROOMS ON THE SECOND FLOOR.

ABOVE: THE MASTER BATHROOM SHARES THE HOUSE'S CALM AND RELAXING ATMOSPHERE. OPPOSITE AND OVERLEAF: THE MASTER BEDROOM IS SURROUNDED BY TREES AND HAS A BALCONY OVERLOOKING A CASCADING MOUNTAIN STREAM.

ACKNOWLEDGMENTS I would like to thank the following people who have made a significant difference in my professional career. Richard Fiore, my husband and collaborator: Your exceptional contracting talents have enabled me to realize my designs fully. You always welcome a challenge, and I look forward to our next adventure: renovating a *petit château* in France. Joseph Lembo, for the joy of working together as a team for so many years. I am proud of what Lembo-Bohn Design Associates was able to achieve and am honored to share our *Interior Design* Hall of Fame award with you. Sara Ledra, Aoife Duffin, and Stephanie Sarkies, all long-time staff at Laura Bohn Design Associates. I could not ask for a more talented team. Cindy Allen, editor-in-chief of *Interior Design*, whose friendship and professional support I treasure. The magazine and the interior design profession are much better because of your untiring advocacy. Jim Bohn, with gratitude for the moral support and inspiration you provided during my years at Pratt Institute, and as a fledgling designer. Joseph D'Urso and Pratt Institute for my exceptional design education. John Saladino, for your inspiring talent and lasting influence. My clients, who through the years have demanded the best of me, and without whose trust and encouragement none of this would have been possible. Wendy Silverstein and WS&A, for your industry, insights, and professional counsel. Very special thanks to Suzanne Slesin of Pointed Leaf Press, who first wrote about me in the Home section of the *New York Times* in 1979. I am grateful to her and her accomplished team—Frederico Farina, Betty Eng, Kelly Koester, and Marion Dreyfus—for providing me new ways of seeing my own life and work. I hope this retrospective serves to both inform and inspire.—Laura Bohn, New York, May, 2017

# INDEX

**LAURA BOHN**, founder of New York–based Laura Bohn Design Associates, is known for creating elegantly modern interiors that combine clean, contemporary lines with deep, practical comfort. A graduate of Pratt Institute, Bohn is a member of the ASID and the *Interior Design* Hall of Fame. She has also taught at Fashion Institute of Technology, Parsons School of Design, and Pratt Institute. Her work is widely published in books and magazines, and is frequently presented on television, where Bohn's low-key charisma and breadth of knowledge lend her compelling authority. Born in Texas, Bohn lives with her husband in New York and Bucks County, Pennsylvania.

**PETER WEBSTER** is an editor, writer, and consultant specializing in design, architecture, men's style, art and culture, and travel. He contributes regularly to *Interior Design* and *Travel + Leisure* magazines among other publications, and has written *The Esquire Handbook of Style* and Taschen's *New New York Interiors*. Webster is a former editor at *Departures*, *House Beautiful*, *Elle Decor*, and *Absolute*, of which he was editor-in-chief. Born in New Zealand, he lives in Brooklyn, New York.

**WENDY SILVERSTEIN** is the founder of WS&A, a New York–based boutique public relations firm specializing in the design, architecture, consumer products, and lifestyle industries. Previously Silverstein spent 20 years working as an editor at *Architectural Digest*, *Home*, and *HomeStyle* magazines. A member of the ASID and IFDA New York Chapters, Silverstein has a degree in architecture from the University of California, Berkeley, and is an IPEC Certified Coach. Born in Los Angeles, she lives in New York with her husband and two daughters.

**PUBLISHER** SUZANNE SLESIN
**MANAGING EDITOR** KELLY KOESTER
**DESIGNER** BETTY ENG

Michel Arnaud: 130-131. Quentin Bacon: 25. Laura Bohn: front endpapers, half-title page, 126-127. Antoine Bootz: 4, 36, 48, 59. Cynthia van Elk: 50-51, 53, 56-57, 60-61. Scott Frances: 38-47. Andrew French: 178, back of back endpapers, back endpapers. David Gilbert: 62-65, 67-70, 72-81, 142-154. John Granen: 154-165. Elliot Kaufman: 118-120, 122-125. Eric Laignel: 21, 29, 30-31, 82-115, 136-141. Marcus Leatherdale: 14. Robert J. Levin: 16-17. Peter Margonelli: cover, 66, 71, 128, 132-135. David O. Marlow: 166-175. Anastassios Mentis: 116, 121. Brandon Rodkewitz: 26. William Waldron: 22-23.

ISBN: 978-1-938461-40-8
Library of Congress Control Number: 2016962162

Printed and Bound in Italy

First Edition. 10 9 8 7 6 5 4 3 2 1

FRONT AND BACK COVERS: A FLOOR-TO-CEILING PARTITION OF PAINTED WOOD SLATS SEPARATES THE FOYER FROM THE SERENE DINING AREA IN A HOUSE I DESIGNED IN BRIARCLIFF MANOR, NEW YORK. FRONT AND BACK OF FRONT ENDPAPERS: I DESIGNED A SHOWER FLOOR OF TEAK SLATS INSET IN MARBLE FOR THE MASTER BATHROOM IN A PURCHASE, NEW YORK, RESIDENCE. OPPOSITE CONTENTS: THE DINING NOOK OF MY MANHATTAN LOFT FEATURES *SWAN*, AN ATMOSPHERIC PAINTING BY AMERICAN ARTIST S AGAIN, ILLUMINATED BY MICHELE DE LUCCHI'S *TOLOMEO* FLOOR LAMP, A MODERN CLASSIC. PAGE 176: FOR A SHOWHOUSE COMMISSIONED BY THE SHOWTIME NETWORK, I WAS ASKED TO DESIGN ROOMS CENTERED AROUND THE TELEVISION SERIES *NURSE JACKIE*. I TURNED THE BATHROOM INTO A CHAPEL REMINISCENT OF THE ONE ON THE SHOW, COMPLETE WITH A SAINTLY HOLOGRAM. BACK OF BACK ENDPAPERS: INSPIRED BY NURSE JACKIE'S PRESCRIPTION-DRUG ADDICTION, I DESIGNED A DISTORTED HOSPITAL ROOM WITH CURTAINS MADE FROM THE SAME LATEX USED IN HOSPITAL GLOVES. BACK ENDPAPERS: THE CHARACTER'S SIGNATURE ADAGE, "LIFE IS A SERIES OF LITTLE PRICKS," DECORATES THE WALLS.

Life is a series of
pricks... Life is a series of little pricks... Life is

a series of little
Life is a series of